VICTORY CRY
Living a resilient life after a birth trauma

Michelle McDonald

Victory Cry: Living a resilient life after a birth trauma

4

Table of Contents

Dedicated

To all the mothers, wives, sisters, daughters, nieces, friends, work colleagues and neighbours who lost their lives through this tragic ordeal that I survived. My hope is that my voice is your echo. It's too hard to stay silent about this.

~

My mother, sister, and husband, who were instrumental in my recovery and by my side the entire time. It was very traumatic for them to see such horrific events unfolding right before their eyes.

~

The doctors and nurses at North York General Hospital in Toronto; namely Dr. Kalpana Sharma, Dr. Lynne Zolis, Dr. Jeremy Wong

Dr. Heather Millar, Dr. Paul Sheun, Dr. Doctor and the pediatric team and all the nurses in ICU and NICU. I can't say enough about their professionalism, dedication and patient care; thank you from the bottom of my heart!

Preface

Victory Cry introduces readers to how a simple yet joyous time in a woman's life like giving birth can leave you with a lifetime scar. Through candid and honest writing and self-reflection, I will turn the nightmare I experienced from an Amniotic Fluid Embolism (AFE) into a bold story of resilience. In fact, through my journey to recovery, I am living an even better life than before!

Here are some insights into Amniotic Fluid Embolism (AFE). It can touch the lives of pregnant mothers of any age, race, religion, social status, your birth order doesn't matter nor does your delivery method. AFE can occur during delivery or shortly after vaginal or cesarean birth, but it is still unclear wha causes AFE, which remains an unpreventable pregnancy complication. AFE is so rare that the statistics around the rate of incidences varies; recent research shows that the estimated incidence in AFE is 1 in 40,000 deliveries in North America and 1 in 53,800 deliveries in Europe. Although AFE is considered rare, research has already shown that AFE is the leading cause of maternal death in Australia and Japan, the second leading cause of maternal death in the United States and United Kingdom, and the third leading cause of maternal death in France and Poland. Estimates on survival rates vary, largely due to poor reporting and the difficulty of diagnosis. However, recent data suggests that 40% of women with AFE will die from it and the mortality rate of infants still in the womb is as high as 65%.

As I share my story of survival, I know that many mothers have experienced various degrees of maternal trauma. I have dedicated this book to help those who might still be feeling the emotional and physical pain, or even survivor's guilt, by trying to remain strong and grasp their new normal. I hope that my experience will birth new life into mothers, causing them to be empowered and shine a light within, that will radiate amongst everyone they meet.

With loving light,
Michelle McDonald

* Statistics sourced from www.afesupport.org

Introduction

This book is written for mothers who are recovering from trauma, but especially a child birth trauma. It is for those who are ready to start seeing results on their journey to recovery. Are you willing to introduce new strategies into your life that can move you in the direction of a more resilient you?

I will be sharing the three important stages of my recovery – stages that I went through and am still going through – on my way to experiencing a resilient life. I hope my journey to recovery will help you discover or ignite your healing. The three stages of my recovery are Reflection, Finding a New Rhythm and A Resilient Life. I'm confident that as you hear more, you will be able to identify where you are on your recovery journey. You'll also learn how to utilize helpful tools and strategies to successfully navigate your way to a state of recovery and resilience.

God brought me through a very difficult and challenging event, and I know he doesn't want me to be silent about it. It's important for me to help who I can, no matter how small the shift may be and rediscover a place of strength, faith, and confidence. It is my greatest hope that after reading this book, you will be encouraged and know that you are alive today for a reason; there is a purpose for your life. You may or may not know what that reason is right now, but please, never for one second feel that you are alone.

Acknowledgement

Steve & Kathy Kidd, along with the team at Kidd Marketing for editing and marketing my book.

Camille Lauren, artist and photographer for capturing the true essence and beauty on the book cover.

Trauma

It is a fact of the human experience that trauma enters our lives, and often when we least expect it. There seem to be few people who escape this life without having something that forever changes who they are. You may have experienced a life-altering situation just as I did. At one point, there you were going about your normal life, when something came up that you did not plan or least expect; an experience that irrevocably changed who you are and how you feel about your life.

I'm happy to tell you there is good news. No matter where you are on your journey, this book can help lead you from where you are right now to somewhere more incredible and wonderful than you could ever imagine. In time, our true essence can shine through trauma, leading us to be the person we're meant to be. So, I encourage you to live your life to the fullest. I challenge you to sing your personal victory cry out loud and continue your quest to a victorious life despite the adversities, and sometimes absurdities of life.

Season of Change

Over the past ten years, I have worked as a corporate meeting planner. I've had an amazing opportunity to collaborate with inspiring and high-profile people. One of the highlights of my professional career was working with the Secretariat for the Governor General's Canadian Leadership Conference. I worked on that project for three consecutive conferences and had the privilege to meet two Governors Generals during that time; The Right Honorable Michaëlle Jean and His Excellency the Right Honorable David Johnston. This was a major highpoint in my career. I'm fortunate to have had a fascinating, impactful and inspiring career but I still didn't feel like I was doing what I was *destined* to do. From as far back as I can remember I've gravitated towards personal growth and development, and regardless of what job I had, I was always seeking to do more and help others realize their true potential.

I was born and raised on the island of Barbados. In 2001, I moved to Canada in search of greater opportunities and to explore what else the world had to offer. During that time, I had a lot of personal growth going on. I'll freely admit I was scared because it was a rollercoaster ride from the very beginning. It was a huge adjustment to move from a small island to a big city and then try to fit into the workplace as a young adult woman who was still growing. Moving through this phase of my life, helped me realized I lacked positive influences. I was having a hard time living in a new country, but I quickly came to realize that my move to Canada was instrumental in helping me grow personally and professionally. I learned how to navigate my way through this new space I now called home and experience many new things at a much faster pace than I was used to. This was definitely not the island way of life I had grown up in! It was at this time that I knew I needed people to help me navigate my new reality.

I'm very grateful for mentors I found online, like Lisa Nichols, for personal growth and transformation, as well as Joyce Meyers, for spiritual growth. These two areas were key for me at the time to keep me grounded and keep growing into the person I was meant to be. Also during this time groups like Toastmasters – District 60 and Speakers Club as well as CAPS (Toronto), enabled me to meet and network with some amazing people and taught me how to speak professionally while improving my leadership skills. These varied groups of people helped me through some of the toughest parts of my journey as young adult life.

More than anything, I've learned in my personal development journey that I always need to draw closer to my spiritual side. My journey has been tough, but at the same time rewarding and fulfilling.

My Survival Story

When my husband and I found out we were expecting our first child, we were absolutely filled with excitement. Having your first baby is a miracle and a privilege. I kept thinking about what he or she would look like! We both decided that we wanted to wait until the birth to know the sex, but as we got closer, the anticipation was bubbling over, and I couldn't contain myself anymore; I just needed to know. Eating healthier was important for me, and I also started practicing yoga to keep me relaxed and calm after those long days at work. Getting my body off to a healthy start was vitally important during my nine-month journey. I was considered a late maternal age for having a child, which only increased my commitment to good health practices. During

21

my pregnancy, I was lucky to experience very few problems, so I planned on having a natural birth. On August 1, 2014, I arrived at the hospital around 6:00 a.m. was checked in and was immediately hooked up to numerous machines to monitor the baby and myself. I was happy to learn that I was already 3 cm. dilated. I couldn't believe this was really happening! Soon, I was given an epidural and was able to rest comfortably. Then, suddenly, I felt a sharp piercing pain in my temples that radiated over parts of my body. I was having difficulty breathing. I asked the nurse to get a doctor as this was nothing like I had ever experienced before. Without prior warning, I felt myself slowly losing consciousness. The last thing I was aware of was doctors and nurses running into the room, calling my name, and hoping I would respond. Then lost all consciousness.

Later, I learned that between my son and I, a total of three emergency codes were announced at the hospital. This was a highly unusual event for one patient. First, there was a code blue called; my doctor immediately thought I was experiencing an amniotic fluid embolism (AFE) based on my symptoms and perhaps I was going into cardiac arrest. I was rushed to the operating room. Then, a code pink was called as the fetal heart rate was very low; so, an emergency cesarean was done and the baby was quickly removed and placed in an incubator. After that, a code omega was called, as there was continuous massive hemorrhaging from my cesarean section.

To save my life, the doctors had to request about 30 units of blood and blood products. In the meantime, to slow down the bleeding, they had to tie off two major arteries on both the right and left side, but I still continued to bleed from the Disseminated Intravascular Coagulation (DIC). I was still unconscious for about 20 hours, then I woke up and was told that I had been diagnosed with something called Amniotic Fluid Embolism/ Disseminated Intravascular Coagulation AFE/DIC. The first phase is AFE - an acute and rapid collapse of mother and baby because of an allergic-like reaction to amniotic fluid entering the maternal circulatory system. The amniotic fluid had leaked into my bloodstream and slowly began poisoning me. The second phase was DIC, which is acute hemorrhaging at the site of an incision. Some women only go through one phase, and some go through both phases like I did. Doctors told me this could happen during or after pregnancy. Ou wonderful, joyous event had been turned int an absolute nightmare. I awoke with a tracheal tube in my throat and was unable to talk. I felt completely disoriented; wondering what happened. I had no idea what time of day it was or where baby Eli was. Was he even alive? Unfortunately, I was alone when I regained consciousness, so my mind began to race with so many negative thoughts. Eventually, my husband walked into the room and sat on the bed. I saw a tear slowly rolling down his cheek. In my brain, I was shouting, "Tell me what happened!" As you could imagine, I needed information quickly. "Don't leave out any details! Where is Eli?!" I shouted at him in my head. Then, pleadingly, in my head, "Please tell me, I want to know." His answers were just taking way too long. After what felt like hours to me, two doctors walked in and began explaining everything that had transpired during my son's delivery.

It was obvious that they were very happy to see me wake up and it was comforting to see their reactions. Their explanation of the unfortunate series of events felt endless; all I wanted to know was if Eli was alright! While they focused on me and my condition, no one realized that as a new mother, all I wanted to know was if my son was alive and healthy. Finally, I was told they had performed an emergency caesarean section, and although Eli was born with very low oxygen, he started improving over the next few hours. It a huge sigh of relief knowing he is alive and doing well. I spent three long days in ICU under close observation before I could be moved to NICU care with Eli for an additional six days before I was discharged.

Of course, Eli was not allowed in the ICU, but I pleaded to see him and my wish wa granted, but they were only able to rest him on my chest for a few seconds. What an amazing moment it was to gaze lovingly at my son for the first time. All I remembered thinking was that he looked like a mini version of my husband!

What just happened?!

I spent three days in ICU were with a tracheal tube in my mouth to keep my airway open and to help assist with administering my medication. This was absolutely the hardest part of my recovery after regaining consciousness. What was most interesting to me though, was that I still didn't know what it felt like to give birth, not even by a cesarean. I didn't get to see my son weighed and measured, nor did I get to give him his first bath. Those simple things are moments of pleasure that new parents look forward to after giving birth. Instead of smelling the top of my baby's head while I snuggled him, I was fighting for my life.

It was very frustrating to only have writing as a form of communication during this delicate time. The benefit of not being able to talk over every detail with my husband, or anyone for that matter, was that it allowed me to be still with myself and my thoughts and just reflect on life. I thought deeply about all that had happened, and even then, I began to plan how I could live life more to the fullest now that I had been given a second chance with my son.

My mom had flown in from Barbados to stay with us the week before Eli was due. The day before I went into the hospital to be induced, we painted each other's toenails and then bought a box of chicken. I sat and ate most of it! Just the thought of, that could have been my last meal, was not a good last impression. It was an understatement to say that I had major cravings that night. In retrospect, I am grateful beyond words that we had my mom there with us. Little did we know then, just how much we would need her and her expertise as a retired nurse.

VICTORY CRY
(Tears of joy)

Home at last! I'll never forget walking into my home again for the first time in nine days. It was surreal for me after all that had unfolded in my life just over a week ago. After all, I expected to be gone for only a day or two and return home with my baby boy in my arms, excited to begin our lives together as a new family. I was very grateful to be home; I felt free, very blessed, and in need of a long, hot bath.

The next four months of my recovery was a humbling experience. As a very independent, persistent and determined woman, I rarely give up on things, but now I was dependent on others, WOW! The dependence was what was most humbling for me. This was not a good feeling, but I needed to learn how to lean on others, in order to heal.

During that first month, I was still extremely weak. I needed help going up or down the stairs. Since I was too weak to breastfeed, I would have Eli lay on the bed next to me or in his bouncer and I would watch him sleep, look at his tiny fingers, feel his soft, smooth skin and play with his hair. With every stroke of my hand, I would thank God again for both us being here together. This joyous moment was my victory cry.

My mother was instrumental in my recovery and in taking care of Eli during the entire four months. As a retired nurse, she was the perfect person you'd want around to help you recover. We were very blessed to have her.

My experiences helped me realize just how frivolous material things are and how precious life is. Most importantly, it drew me closer to God and helped me strengthen my faith in Him. He gave me another chance at life and made me realize I was here for a bigger reason; to do more and serve a bigger purpose. I came to the realization that anything could happen at any time. I got to a place where I was able to focus on just how grateful I was for every moment. For some people following a traumatic experience, the awareness of the tenuous nature of life is unsettling and even frightening. But for me, it instilled a deeper sense of gratitude in my soul.

Most of us experience trauma in varying degrees. It may be related to your health or something else, but your traumatic experience is no less impactful on your life than anyone else's. When you know you have made it out safely from your awful experience, I hope you will let out your own victory cry. Just as each of us is unique, so too is our personal victory cry. My victory cry arose from developing a greater capacity for love, inner peace, self-confidence and faith in my Creator.

You've heard my story, now replace the content of my story with your own traumatic experience. Include all the details you remember, including your emotions and the sensory effects that go along with your story. This may be painful but owning your trauma is a necessary step towards recovery. Your experience may still be fresh in your mind, or it may have happened a few months or years ago. You've probably told your story many times but may still feel like nobody tru understands your situation. If you're still in the healing process and the recovery stage, this is probably true. However, I assure you that you will eventually realize that you have the ability to love more, be more confident and become more resilient than you could ever imagine. You *can* live in a state of peace or enlightenment that you did not even know was possible because you've come through adversity that has not only altered your life but has blessed it as well.

Whenever you think of your situation and all the obstacles that you've had to overcome, you'll have your own victory cry. I encourage you to stop and look at where you are today, right now. No matter where you are in your recovery journey and what you have come through so far, you are not alone. It might not be an easy road, but I'll be here to help you through each stage. I want you to move from the traumatic or adverse experience that many of us so often define ourselves by, into a state of resilience. Your resilient life will be born from your victory cry.

The 3 R's to Recovery

"Our deepest fear is not that we are inadequate. Our deepest fear is that we are powerful beyond measure. It is our light, not our darkness that most frightens us. We ask ourselves, "Who am I to be brilliant, gorgeous, talented, and fabulous?" Actually, who are you not to be? You are a child of God. Your playing small does not serve the world. There is nothing enlightened about shrinking so that other people won't feel insecure around you. We are all meant to shine, as children do. We were born to make manifest the glory of God that is within us. It's not just in some of us; it's in everyone. And as we let our own light shine, we unconsciously give other people permission to do the same. As we are liberated from our own fear, our presence automatically liberates others."
~ Marianne Williamson

I started this chapter with one of my favorite quotes. It speaks powerfully about who we are at this very moment, not just who we can be.

37

It speaks to who you can become once you have started to overcome your traumatic experience. Every time I read this quote, it inspires me to keep going and never to let my dreams die. You have everything you need right inside of you; you just need to tap into it, and you will see how bright your light will shine. Many of us fall into a trap after an injury or illness and blame ourselves. When we begin to regain strength, we may even feel that we are unworthy of recovery. But the truth is that there is beauty and magic in understanding that we are resilient. Being resilient allows us to persevere and get up to face a new day. In your own time, working through all that pain and suffering is essential to realizing the vibrant health and wellness you were designed for. We are the very face of the glory of God at this moment!

Resilience may be about bouncing back to your original form, but I know that you can come back better, stronger and more empowered than before your traumatic experience. Why? Because it has been my experience; it can be your experience too.

Where do I go from here? Well, I would like to help you transition through the three stages of recovery like I did. Just remember that you are a brilliant and divine being just as you are right now. Sometimes it is hard to remember that we have a purpose, especially as mothers, even when we feel broken or weak. Have a grateful spirit of where you are today, with this gift of the present you can grow a little bit more than before. Each day builds on the other, all of them collective building blocks and stepping stones towards recovery.

Stage One:
REFLECTION

The first stage is reflection. My reflection began by trying to process my thoughts about certain things, such as what would have happened if I had not survived? I would have never met my son or seen him grow up. I kept thinking about the last conversation I had with my husband and mother. While in the hospital, my husband and mother had been discussing what to eat. I remember being quiet even though I was very hungry. Those are some snippets of thoughts that continually ran through my mind. But there was one overriding thought above all others. Why had my life been spared, or, you may call survivors guilt? It might seem strange that thought so much about that one thing. Perhaps I should have just been grateful to be alive and moved on. But somehow, I knew that question deserved my time and pondering. I felt very grateful, and I also felt that I had a greater purpose and bigger mission to fulfill. Clearly, my work here on this earth was not done! Another memory I had was that my husband and I were setting up life insurance policies. We wanted to get it all completed before the baby came, but there were delays in signing the policy, so I didn't actually have life insurance coverage when I went into deliver our baby. Imagine that!

It's amazing how my mind and thoughts have shifted since my experience. I don't feel like the same person that I was before, physically or emotionally. It took me some time to embrace the fact that it is perfectly okay for me to not feel like the same person I was. After all, how could you go through all that, and just return to being the same person you were before?   So, even as I found myself slipping back to wondering about my old life, I knew that this path was leading me to where I was supposed to be.   When I emerge fully healed, I will be the person I am meant to be. My gift is to show up in the world with that "thing" that I was uniquely meant to bring into the world.

Building and maintaining self-confidence after a traumatic experience can be one of the biggest challenges in your recovery. Trauma isn't just about the physical impact. Trauma impacts us in every way; physically, spiritually, and emotionally. This opens up portal for negative images and negative self talk to gain a foothold in our very being

Clearing away self-doubt takes practice; you can't do it in just one sitting. You'll need to replace those negative thoughts and feelings with positive ones. We've all heard that there are no vacuums in nature. If we remove something in this case, like self-doubt we need to replace it with something positive.

I worked on regaining my confidence by acknowledging what I had been through, then by embracing that I'm still here. I had to start building myself up and finding the courage within to take the next step to grow, move on, and do more. There is something profound that shakes you to your soul when you experience a trauma of the depth that I experienced. For some reason, you doubt yourself and your strength after it is over. Sometimes you doubt your abilities and decisions. It takes time to regain your footing and trust in your own confidence. We want to get better, all at once, but recovery is a process and a time to be gentle with ourselves. Think of recovery as a marathon, not a sprint. Each step forward builds on the last, and even when we don't feel it, we are making progress.

Stage Two:
Finding a New RHYTHM

The second stage is about transitioning from my reflection state to becoming more independent. There will be days when you just don't feel like getting up and doing anything. But those are the days that you need to move and push yourself gently. As a new mother, you have a little person(s) whom you are responsible for and is depending on you. If you already have children or even if this is your first child, finding that place within to feel fulfillment and to be in a peak state is where it all begins. It took me a couple of weeks after my recovery to find my new rhythm. Finding about thirty minutes in the morning just for me, before my day really started with my son, was essential.

Then I started to think about which of my basic human needs were not being met now that this tragic event was over. After pondering this for a while, it felt like I needed it all right then, but there was one thing that I was lacking the most and that was growth/progress. This experience caused me to search for what this thing called AFE was all about, it really made me open my eyes to what could really happen, and what I had never heard about before. I needed to tell someone, anyone that would listen.

That's when I knew I couldn't stay silent about this; I had to determine what I wanted my outcome to be like. That's when I started with a short video, and I decided to write a book sharing my personal story, with the hope that my story will help other mothers heal from their traumatic experience.

We hear about people saying that it's all about getting back to how your life was before the trauma. Maybe for you it will be more about how to get to the life that you were *meant* to have now that you've come through the trauma. Life doesn't have to be how it was before. It can be a whole lot better!

Let's say you're not moving forward because you care too much about what other people think. This can refer to the lack of self-confidence that we talked about in the reflection stage. Because we are still having negative thoughts about ourselves, we can place too much importance on the opinions of others. I encourage you to focus on the fact that no one truly knows what you've come through. No one knows what it's been like for you physically or emotionally. It's okay just to be you. It's okay to move at your own pace.

Pleasing *you* and listening to yourself and your body should be your top priority to help you along your journey to recovery. There will be people who are going to be there for you, and there will be people who won't. Let those who can't or won't support you, go, and focus on the special people who are there for you now. This can be a tipping point if you allow it. It can be difficult to face losing someone who was important to you on top of everything else you have been through. Shifting you focus to the positive people in your life is key. Let them know how important they are to you and your recovery. Show them gratitude and thanks for their support. Your words of gratitude may very well be received at the moment they need it to hear it most. The best relationships are ones that are in balance. At this point, you may not physically be strong enough to do many good deeds for others, but you can always show your gratitude.

Developing a stronger spiritual connection with God will be pivotal; He will become your anchor. Your trauma will help you see that there is something greater than you. Reach out and allow yourself to be connected to that energy. Take some quiet time and be still, and know that God has brought you to this place in your life, and He can take you through anything. We only have to let go and let Him guide us through our toughest moments. You just have to get to know Him. Spend time with Him by praying, and embrace the fact that God has set a purpose for your life.

As you begin to truly understand yourself, keep a positive thought pattern and as you align your emotional state, you will start to find your new rhythm. You will start empowering yourself to move forward. Who knows? Your new life rhythm may lead you in a new direction entirely. This rhythm can be found when you are in silence and tapping into your power center and you are aligned with how you are feeling.

Stage Three:
A RESILIENT LIFE

You have moved from a reflection state to a state of independence and moving towards interdependence. Now you can stand taller and stronger with your feet planted firmly on the ground. This will allow you to be more confident in your skin, and by doing so, helping others do the same. Remember that you are influencing the growth of others simply by continuing to work on your own recovery. It may be your children, spouse, parents, siblings, friends or colleagues. You are being admired and respected for your resilience. People will be watching how you have recovered with so much life and vigor. This will be your opportunity to shine because you have rebuilt your life on a whole new foundation, with so many wonderful people surrounding you. Your faith in God is stronger, and you know that nothing can shake you, especially with positive thinking, aligned with your emotional state as you take action. This is when a radical shift will take place in your life.

With your pure heart, continue to show love and kindness to others while respecting your boundaries. This will reap high rewards that will continue to grow and become very successful.

Most of my friends will tell you that I'm a positive, determined and upbeat person. However, I will still have bad days, we all do. Rebuilding your life does not suddenly make you immune to the daily bumps and bruises that we all experience. You will get knocked down from time to time, but now you know how to dust yourself off and get back up with even more resilience than before. Every bad experience can teach us something when we allow it. Know that life's lessons may not always be immediately revealed, but the important thing is not to dwell on the problem; learn from it and keep moving forward.

Shift your focus to your personal goals, set up an action plan and stay on track towards achieving them. When things don't happen in the time you think they should, reflect on the fact that it will happen in its proper time. Don't worry about what others may have to say about your recovery timeline. There is always so much more going on behind the scenes; much like a successful event. As the attendee, you see the final result: the beautiful décor, smell the delicious food and listen to the wonderful music. As an experienced corporate meeting planner, I know that there are dozens of moving parts and pieces that have to be orchestrated in a very specific way to pull off the perfect event. Your recovery is a bit like that. Only you know all the pieces that need to be coordinated each day. Most people mean well, but their good intentions can derail you sometimes if you let them. Just smile, thank them for their concern and honor your own timeline. Even on the days that you feel you have not progressed, or perhaps even regressed, there is important work being done. Some days there may be more of an emotional recovery, and other days it may be more in the physical realm. But each day as you honor yourself and do the work, good things will surely start happening.

Remember you were given a second or perhaps even a third chance at life. Don't waste another moment; someone desperately needs to hear your story. Your story doesn't end with the details of your trauma. Inspiration comes from what we do with our story. What will you do with yours? What will be your victory cry?

Celebrate your life

Come, let's celebrate your life. Everyday we need to celebrate even the little accomplishments. It could be as small as getting your child potty trained; putting your child to bed on-time without any resistance or even when they turn to you and say, "Mommy I love you." That's the best feeling ever!

I would love to share with you more about the three stages of recovery and how they can be applied to your life. The coaching programs I have developed will take you through each stage - Reflection, Rhythm, and Resilience, showing you how to create a life of excellence from your personal experiences.

My life coaching services are available one-or one or in a group setting. For more information, please visit my Facebook page at www.facebook.com/resiliencyliving or my website at www.michellemcdonald.ca

My Favorite Quotes

"Sometimes you have to be willing to let go of something old to grab onto something new. You have to be willing to let a part of you die that you used to be comfortable with in order for another part of you to be born."
~ Lisa Nichols

"If you don't like something, change it. If you can't change it, change your attitude. Don't complain." ~ Maya Angelou

"When there is light in the soul, there is beauty in the person. When there is beauty in the person, there is harmony in the house. When there is harmony in the house, there is order in the nation. When there is order in the nation there is peace in the world."
~ Chinese Proverb

"Love is a willing self-sacrifice for the good of another that does not require reciprocation or that the person being loved is deserving."
~Paul Tripp

"I've learned that people will forget what you said, people will forget what you did, but people will never forget how you made them feel." ~Maya Angelou

"When your clarity meets your conviction, and you apply action to the equation, your world will begin to transform before your eyes." ~Lisa Nichols

"The thing you fear most has no power. Your fear of it is what has the power. Facing the truth really will set you free." ~Oprah Winfrey

"Always stay true to yourself and never let what someone else says distract you from your goals." ~ Michelle Obama

Short Prayer Starters
by Joyce Meyer

Dear God, even though I don't always feel like it, life tries to get me to quit, I believe that you have a great plan for my life. I choose to trust you to help me live the dreams you have given me more than I trust my circumstances. Amen

Dear God, you are all I need. Help me not to trust in myself, but to put my trust in you and to rely only on you. I believe that you are at work in my life, even during difficult times. I choose today to remain steadfast and to never give up in obedience to you. Amen

Dear God, I want to be able to say that I have completed the work you have for me. Thank you for working in me to give me the power and the desire to live for your pleasure and finish my course with joy! Everyday there is another opportunity that you have given me to reach out, bless and influence someone else with your love. I want to live a life of blessing towards others, showing them what means to live a God-focused life. Amen.

Dear God, remind me to bring my problems to you. I'm tired of living in my own strength. I need your guidance and your direction. As I seek you daily, I will put my trust in you. Lead me into your peace that passes all understanding. Show me the daily steps I can take to walk in your peace for me. Amen.

Dear God, I want to be content and satisfied with where I am, right here, right now. Give me the strength to choose to be content every single day. I want my contentment to come from you, not my circumstances. Show me every day that your plan for me is perfect and that I don't need to worry. Amen

Dear God, I know that true happiness comes from giving, not receiving. I want to live the life of true happiness that comes from forgetting about my selfish desires and seek to give to those around me. Amen

Dear God, sometimes the situation in front of me seems impossible, but you have brought me through difficult times in the past, and I know you can do it again. Help me to remember past successes and to think positively about my present situation. Amen.

Dear God, I can't just sit back any longer, waiting for peace to materialize. I want to actively pursue it. Show me the way as I go after your peace. Help me take an inventory of my life and cut out pointless activities. I don't want to be too busy. Show me how to live a more fruitful life. Amen.

74647559R00036

Made in the USA
Columbia, SC
07 August 2017